TIMES PAST
SOUTH
YORKSHIRE

Top, left to right: **Birdcage Lodge, Clifton Park, Rotherham, 1900; Peel Square, Barnsley, early 1900s; buffer girls, Sheffield, *c* 1910; Bottom: Market Place, Doncaster, *c* 1900.**

MELVYN JONES

MYRIAD
LONDON

Local landmarks

South Yorkshire is dotted from west to east with memorable landmarks dating from every century since early medieval times. They include castles, public buildings, church towers and spires, monuments, follies, great or interesting houses and unusual structures. They are places that remain in the memory of people who have long left the region; and, for those that remain, they are sometimes useful meeting places

ABOVE: **OBSERVATION TOWER, LOCKE PARK, BARNSLEY**, *c* 1910. The tower was a gift by Miss Sarah McCreery in memory of her sister, Mrs Phoebe Locke. Mrs Locke had presented the land for Locke Park, opened in 1862, in memory of her late husband, Joseph Locke, the railway engineer.

LEFT: **BARNSLEY TOWN HALL, MID-1930S.** Constructed in 1932-33, of white limestone blocks, this imposing Classical Revival-style building was designed by the Liverpool architects, Briggs & Thornely. It replaced the dingy old Town Hall in St Mary's Gate and cost £188,000 to build and furnish.

BELOW: **SHEFFIELD CITY HALL.** Opened in 1932, it was originally designed as early as 1920 by E Vincent Harris. It is built in the Classical Revival-style dominated by a portico with eight Corinthian columns. Originally conceived as a memorial hall for the city's First World War dead it became Sheffield's main concert hall.

CLOCK CORNER. DONCASTER.

ABOVE: **CLOCK CORNER, DONCASTER, 1920S.** This view is from St Sepulchre Gate towards Baxter Gate. On the left is Clock Corner (Oriel Chambers, constructed 1894) and on the right the green-topped dome of the York City & Commercial Bank (1898), later Midland Bank and now HSBC.

RIGHT: **ST GEORGE'S CHURCH, DONCASTER, c 1905.** This fine Victorian church is seen in the distance from the banks of the Sheffield & South Yorkshire Navigation. It was completed in 1858 by Sir Gilbert Scott to replace the medieval St Mary's, destroyed in a fire.

Parish Church from the Don, Doncaster.

BELOW: **KEPPEL'S COLUMN, c 1920.** This 115ft (35m) high obelisk, completed in 1782, was built to commemorate the acquittal of Admiral Augustus Keppel, a close friend and ally of the 2nd Marquis of Rockingham of Wentworth Woodhouse. Keppel had been accused of failing to engage the French fleet in 1778.

THE MUSEUM, CLIFTON PARK, ROTHERHAM

E.L.S 172-138. Keppel's Column, Near Rotherham

ABOVE: **CLIFTON PARK MUSEUM, ROTHERHAM, EARLY 1900S.** This house, in Clifton Park, dates from the 1780s and was originally the home of Joshua Walker, son of Samuel Walker, one of the founders of Masbrough Iron Foundry. It became a museum in 1893.

ABOVE: **CHAPEL ON THE BRIDGE, ROTHERHAM, c 1890.** This is one of only four bridge chapels still surviving in England. It was constructed in the late 15th century and travellers could give their thanks for their safe arrival in the town or pray for a safe journey when leaving it.

STREET SCENES

All the four major urban centres in South Yorkshire were transformed in the 19th and early 20th centuries by industrial expansion, accompanied by explosive population growth not only in the urban centres themselves but also in the villages and small towns in their hinterlands. This rapidly changing situation is reflected in these street scenes

ABOVE: **FARGATE, SHEFFIELD, 1920S.** The view of Fargate on a busy weekday is from high up in the Town Hall, with the *Sheffield Telegraph* building in the distance and the spire of St Marie's Roman Catholic cathedral on the right.

LEFT: **FITZALAN SQUARE, SHEFFIELD, EARLY 1900S.** The square was then a busy tram terminus. The building in the centre background is the Fitzalan Market Hall. The building with a dome and classical columns is the office of the Birmingham, Dudley and District Bank.

RIGHT: **MOORHEAD, SHEFFIELD, EARLY 1900S.** The photograph shows the view looking along Pinstone Street towards the Town Hall on the right. In the left foreground is Roberts Brothers' department store built in 1882 and destroyed by German bombs on December 12 1940.

ABOVE: **CHEAPSIDE, BARNSLEY, 1912.** "Cheapside" is from the Anglo-Saxon word *cieping* meaning a market. In 1912 it was flanked on one side by shops and on the other by the market on May Day Green. The flags and banners are for the visit of King George V and Queen Mary.

RIGHT: **QUEEN STREET, BARNSLEY, *c* 1910.** The view is south-eastwards along Queen Street towards the market stalls on May Day Green. Of special interest are the two mill-workers characteristically wearing shawls, probably power loom weavers at one of the town's linen mills.

Right: **HIGH STREET, WOMBWELL, EARLY 1900s.** High Street was Wombwell's main business thoroughfare with a town hall, market place, three banks and a wide selection of retail shops including, most prestigious of all, branch No 3 of the Barnsley British Co-operative Society (left foreground).

Below: **LOWER MILLGATE, ROTHERHAM, 1880s.** The view is from the west bank of the River Don to Millgate and the crowded and smoky late Victorian town dominated by All Saints' Church. Rebuilt in the late Middle Ages, it is generally regarded as one of the most magnificent parish churches in Yorkshire.

Above: **FRENCH GATE, DONCASTER, c 1930.** It is 3.15pm on a busy shopping day. On the left-hand side can be seen Jackson's Stores and further down the street the Guildhall and Fox's music shop. In the right foreground is the Electra, the town's first purpose-built cinema.

Above: **ST SEPULCHRE GATE, DONCASTER, c 1910.** The early professional photographer with his tripod and black sheet always attracted the attention of a crowd of children and passers-by. Beyond the shops protected from the summer sun by their blinds rises the tower of St George's Church.

The industrial workshop

Manufacturing, particularly metal-processing industries, became the major employer of labour in South Yorkshire in the 19th and early 20th centuries. The light steel trades and heavy steel and engineering industries of Sheffield were complemented by iron, steel and brass founding industries in Rotherham and Barnsley and their surrounding areas and by railway engineering in Doncaster

RIGHT: **SHEFFIELD PEN-KNIFE GRINDERS**, *c* 1900. Grinders put the cutting edge on cutlery and other edge tools at grindstones powered by water or steam power. For centuries they suffered early deaths caused by "grinders' asthma" as a result of inhaling stone and metal dust.

FAR RIGHT: **AXLE FORGE, STEEL, PEECH & TOZER**, 1953. The photograph shows the axle forge at the Icles works in Rotherham. Better known for its Templeborough steelworks, the firm came into existence in 1875 as Steel, Tozer and Hampton to manufacture steel rails for the railways.

INTERIOR CRUCIBLE FURNACE "TEEMING."

LEFT: **CRUCIBLE SHOP, SHEFFIELD, EARLY 1900S.** The development of crucible steel-making by watch and clockmaker Benjamin Huntsman in the 1740s resulted in the worldwide renown of Sheffield cutlery and an international reputation for Sheffield as a steel-making centre.

BELOW: **HEAVY CASTINGS FOUNDRY AT NEWTON CHAMBERS, EARLY 1950S.** This photograph at Thorncliffe Ironworks was taken by Walter Nurnberg (1907-1991), the founding father of modern industrial photography. He used a Rolleiflex camera with powerful lamps to create strong dramatic scenes.

ABOVE: **BLAST FURNACES, NEWTON CHAMBERS**, *c* 1890. Pig iron was made by Newton Chambers at their Thorncliffe Ironworks from 1795 to 1942. The blast furnaces shown here were erected in 1873-74 to replace the two that had been built in 1795 and 1796.

LEFT: **CAMMELL-LAIRD STEELWORKS, PENISTONE, EARLY 1920S.** Steelworks lined the banks of the River Don from Kilnhurst to Penistone, a distance of 15 miles. Cammell-Laird came to Penistone in 1863. As part of the English Steel Corporation, the works closed in 1930.

BELOW: **SAMUEL FOX'S, STOCKSBRIDGE, 1920S.** Stocksbridge was created in 1842 when Samuel Fox opened a wire-drawing plant there. Crinoline wire and umbrella frames made Fox his first fortune and the manufacture of steels rails his second. The plant still survives.

ABOVE: **BAKER AND BESSEMER'S, KILNHURST,** *c* **1930.** Founded in 1874, this firm's first site was at Conisbrough and it then moved to the Brinsworth Works in Rotherham. The Kilnhurst site was purchased in 1903 and the plant operated until 1963. The firm made tramway and railway wheels and axles.

RIGHT: **FLYING SCOTSMAN, DONCASTER, 1924.** The Flying Scotsman was designed by Sir Nigel Gresley and built at the Doncaster Works in 1923 at a cost of £7,944. It was the first locomotive to break through the 100mph barrier which it did in 1934.

KING COAL

In 1900 there were more than 60 collieries in South Yorkshire. In 1908 the first colliery was sunk on the concealed coalfield and this heralded a further expansion of the industry in the east of the region. In 1970 there were still nearly 50 collieries in production employing more than 50,000 miners. Today there are just two collieries employing less than 1,000 men

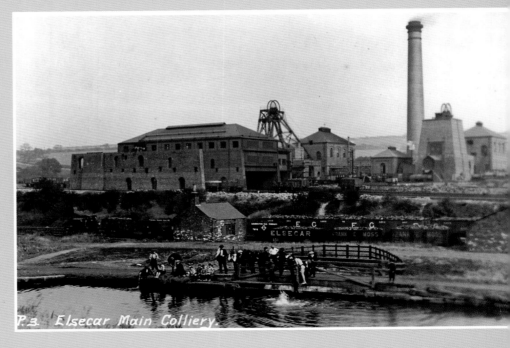

P.3. Elsecar Main Colliery.

ABOVE: **ELSECAR MAIN COLLIERY,** *c* **1920.** Elsecar Main Colliery, one of Earl Fitzwilliam's collieries, was sunk in 1908. It succeeded Simon Wood Colliery (sunk in 1853) which was also a successor to an earlier colliery, Elsecar Colliery, that was already in existence in 1750.

BELOW: **TANKERSLEY COLLIERY,** *c* **1900.** This colliery, owned by Newton Chambers, was closed in 1927. In January 1870 it was attacked by a large number of armed, striking miners wanting to intimidate "blackleg" miners. They broke windows, smashed lamps and hurled coal wagons down the shaft.

ABOVE: **COAL SCREENS, BARNSLEY MAIN COLLIERY,** *c* **1910.** One of the first jobs on taking up employment in a pit and often the last one before retiring was working in the screens, sorting the coal by size and removing "dross" before it was loaded into coal wagons.

BELOW: **HUSKAR PIT MONUMENT.** This memorial in Silkstone churchyard commemorates the death of 26 children who worked in the pit and who were drowned when the pit flooded in 1838. The victims were seven girls aged from eight to 17 and 15 boys aged from seven to 16.

RIGHT: **ROCKINGHAM COLLIERY,** *c* **1910.** Rockingham Colliery between Hoyland and Birdwell was sunk between 1873-75 by Newton Chambers of Thorncliffe. It had 170 coke ovens, seen in the foreground, erected in 1883. One of the by-products of coke-making at Rockingham was the famous disinfectant, Izal.

LEFT: **NEW ROSSINGTON, 1930s.** This photograph shows part of one of the well laid-out 20th-century planned coal-mining settlements on the concealed coalfield in the Doncaster area. Typically the streets are laid out in geometrical designs on Garden City principles.

BELOW: **LONG ROW, CARLTON, c 1910.** In contrast to the large, planned mining settlements built in the 20th century were the simple ones built in the form of long terraced rows, often next to the pit gates. The Long Row accommodated miners working at Wharncliffe Woodmoor 4 and 5 (New Carlton) Colliery.

ABOVE: **SNAP TIME AT GRANGE COLLIERY, KIMBERWORTH, 1940s.** "Snap" was the food and drink eaten by miners in their break. In 1841 a Government report stated that they had "bread, and sometimes bread and meat, or bread and cheese". With the addition of a drink of cold tea nothing much had changed by the 1940s.

LEFT: **LOCK-OUT AT KILNHURST COLLIERY, 1906.** Mining disputes were often long and hard. The 1984 national miners' strike of 18 months was matched by one of similar length at the collieries of Newton Chambers in 1869-70. In the 19th century striking miners were often evicted from their homes.

ABOVE: **CELEBRATION DINNER, MALTBY MAIN COLLIERY, JULY 9 1910.** The 7ft (2m) thick Barnsley Seam was reached at Maltby Main Colliery on June 17 1910 at a depth of 820 yards (750m), hence the celebrations. This colliery was one of the first of the collieries on the concealed coalfield.

LEFT: **BENTLEY COLLIERY.** Located 2½ miles north of Doncaster, Bentley Colliery was also one of the earliest collieries on the concealed coalfield. A decision was made to sink the colliery in 1902, but because of technical difficulties it did not come into production until 1910. It closed in 1993.

EVERYDAY LIFE

In the late 19th and early 20th centuries when these photographs were taken everyday life in South Yorkshire was very different from today. It was a world of coal fires, peggy tubs, washboards and outdoor privies, and of families who were affected by two world wars. There was no television, no superstores, no computers and most people did not have a telephone. The good old days!

LEFT: **SWEET PEA ROW, BURNCROSS NEAR CHAPELTOWN, EARLY 1900S.** The local community pose outside their homes. It is Sunday morning, the menfolk are at home, the children dressed for chapel, and the smell of Yorkshire puddings wafts from the open doorways.

BELOW: **WOODBURN ROAD, WESLEYAN REFORM CHAPEL, ATTERCLIFFE, 1912.** Loaves are being distributed to the wives of striking miners. The strike was a minimum wage dispute that involved all the coalfields. The miners in this case probably worked at the nearby Nunnery Colliery.

LEFT: **FIRTH PARK, SHEFFIELD, 1905.** The photograph shows the ornamental pond in the park, which was donated by steel magnate Mark Firth. It was recorded in the 1890s that as many as 1,000 people visited the park every day in spring and summer.

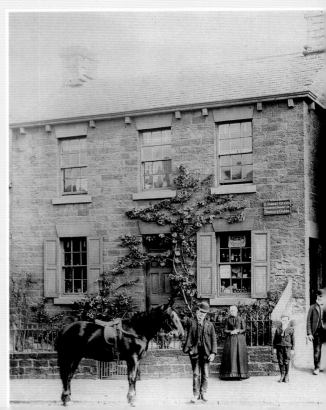

ABOVE: **HORSE BUS, SHEFFIELD, 1880S.** Horse buses came into operation in 1838 from the Moor and Glossop Road to link with the Bridgehouses railway station on the Sheffield to Rotherham railway that opened in that year.

RIGHT: **SMALL SHOP, KINGSTONE, BARNSLEY, *c* 1900.** A shopkeeping family, with their saddle horse, pose outside their shop at Kingstone. The shop belongs to Robert Oakes, licensed dealer in tobacco and cigars. Period clues include the bowler hats, the sailor suit and the shuttered windows.

LEFT: **SCHOLES, 1906.** A smart turn-out, with pinafores for the girls and caps for the boys. In 1891 the population of the village was 328, and out of a male working population of 102, no fewer than 88 were coalminers.

ABOVE: **MARTHA CHESMAN OF THORPE HESLEY, 1920S.** The photograph was taken by William Chesman, miner and part-time village photographer, of his mother Martha who died in 1929. What is unusual about the photograph is its setting – the interior of a working-class family's cottage with its stone sink, cast-iron kitchen range and clothes hanging on a line above the fire.

ABOVE: **PIG KILLER, HOWBROOK, _c_ 1900.** Amos Dransfield, the pig killer, stands on the left wearing an apron. He was a miner who lived in neighbouring High Green. Nothing was wasted: products included chitterlings, roast pig chaps, bacon, ham, pig's feet and hocks, lard and brawn.

RIGHT: **LOWER MILLGATE, ROTHERHAM, LATE 1870S.** This early photograph shows a group of cottages and workshops huddled together between the River Don and the parish church. Before slum clearance, the mixture of residential, industrial and commercial buildings in a polluted atmosphere was a fact of life for many townspeople.

RIGHT: **FRANK CAFFREY'S CYCLE SHOP, DONCASTER ROAD, BARNSLEY, *c* 1910.** The cycling craze of the 1890s had been joined by the time this photograph was taken by the popularisation of the motorcycle. Frank Caffrey sold bicycles and BSA motorcycles (which had been in production since 1903).

BELOW: **HARLEY POST OFFICE AND GROCERY STORE, EARLY 1900S.** Standing proudly beside a tempting window display full of bottles and jars, the sub-postmaster and his two assistants, wearing newly-washed aprons, look ready to face a busy day.

LEFT: BRIDGEGATE, ROTHERHAM, *c* 1910. This photograph of Bridgegate, a busy shopping street, which led from the bridge over the River Don to the parish church, was taken before it was widened between 1914-28. It is barely wide enough for a wheeled vehicle to rumble over its cobbles.

BELOW: MARKET PLACE, DONCASTER, 1890S. The photographer who set up his tripod to take this quiet street scene soon gathered a group to pose against the window of Beetham's wine & spirit merchants, and possibly the proud owner of the bulging Boys' Clothing Warehouse on the right.

BOTTOM: ARP WARDENS, RAMSDEN ROAD, ROTHERHAM, 1940. These ARP (air raid patrol) wardens would patrol at night during the Second World War looking for the slightest chink of light. "Put that ruddy light out" was an often yelled instruction.

LEFT: STREET SCENE, DONCASTER, *c* 1900. Children pose at their doors in a terraced street. There are no front gardens but a covered passage (known in South Yorkshire as a "ginnel" or "jennel") leads to a communal backyard probably with shared privies. A chimney sweep, James Butterfield, lives in the nearest house.

BELOW: COTTAGE SCENE, CHAPELTOWN, 1930S. After the day's shift at Newton Chambers' ironworks this worker has a quiet smoke beside a Yorkshire range in his cottage kitchen while the kettle boils for a strong cup of tea.

Leisure and pleasure

Except for trips to the coast to Bridlington, Scarborough, Cleethorpes and Blackpool, most people's leisure time was spent locally until about 40 years ago. Nearby dams and reservoirs provided a substitute for the sea, there were town and village galas and feasts, excursions to local parks and to the surrounding countryside, team games to play and watch and, as a special treat, a day out at Doncaster races

ECCLESFIELD HOSPITAL PARADE, JUNE 19TH, 1909.

ABOVE: **ECCLESFIELD HOSPITAL PARADE, 1909.** In the days before the National Health Service hospitals relied for much of their money on bequests, endowments and public generosity. In Ecclesfield parades were held between 1898 and 1936. The decorated carts were accompanied by collectors armed with buckets to collect the money.

RIGHT: **CHARABANC OUTING, *c* 1910.** Outings to the Peak District, Sherwood Forest, to a race meeting or to the seaside became extremely popular with the emergence of the charabanc. This is a trip from the High Greave Hotel, Ecclesfield.

ABOVE: **SEASIDE STUDIO PORTRAIT, 1890s.** One for the family album! "Dressed to the nines", members of the Greaves family of Cross Hill, Ecclesfield, hold their poses in a photographic studio while on holiday in Blackpool.

RIGHT: **WHIT GATHERING OF HIGH GREEN AND CHAPELTOWN CHURCHES AND CHAPELS, 1930.** Thousands were involved in the Whit Sings when hymns that had been practised for many weeks beforehand would be sung with great gusto. This one was held in the Ten Acre field with Thorncliffe Ironworks forming a dramatic backdrop.

Left: Old Stand and Pavilion, Bramall Lane. Bramall Lane was originally a cricket ground. Yorkshire County Cricket Club was founded in Sheffield in 1863 and county matches were played at Bramall Lane for more than a century. It became Sheffield United's football ground in 1889.

Below: Otter swimming team, Sheffield, early 1900s. Swimming teams were formed after the opening of public swimming baths. The first Sheffield Corporation swimming baths were opened in 1869 and in 1895 they took over Glossop Road swimming and Turkish baths that had been opened in 1836.

Manor Baths, Askern

Left: Askern Lake near Doncaster, early 1900s. Askern Lake or Pool was recorded as early as 1370-71. By 1814 it had become a place of "great resort" for health and pleasure. A pump house was built and it became one of the "watering places of the north".

Below: Elsecar by the sea, early 1950s. The reservoir-side location of Elsecar Park attracted the title of "Elsecar by the Sea" by the beginning of the 20th century. Bathing and boating on the reservoir became a favourite summer pastime. You could even buy Elsecar rock!

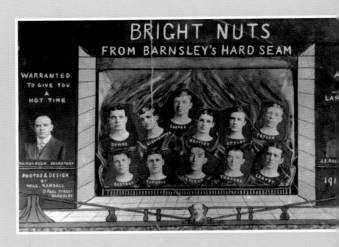

Above: **DRINKING FOUNTAIN, LOCKE PARK, BARNSLEY, EARLY 1900S.** This fountain started life in Peel Square but was moved to the park in October 1866. It had been purchased by the Sunday School Band of Hope Union. The aim was to deter the thirsty from visiting a public house!

TOP RIGHT: **BARNSLEY, FA CUP-WINNERS, 1912.** A clever photographic montage of Barnsley's FA Cup-winning team of 1912, relating them to the coalfield in which the team was located. They won 1-0 after extra time in a replay against West Bromwich Albion after a 0-0 draw.

RIGHT: **CYCLISTS OUTSIDE WENTWORTH PARK, EARLY 1900S.** The lanes around Wentworth provided pleasant and quiet routes for Edwardian cyclists from the surrounding towns and industrial villages, and the lodge gates at the entrance to the park were attractive backdrops for group photographs.

LEFT: **OLYMPIA SKATING RINK, BARNSLEY, c 1910.** The Olympia Skating Rink was opened in 1909. In 1920 it became a cinema, the Pavilion, known by its patrons as "The Pav". In its early days the cinema had its own symphony orchestra. It was destroyed in a disastrous fire in 1950.

RIGHT: **TICKHILL GALA, 1913.** A large crowd of onlookers, in every type of headgear imaginable, inspect this horse-drawn float of North American Indians and their tepee. A sign of the times is that someone in the crowd is holding a "Votes for Women" placard.

Above: Doncaster racecourse. Hundreds of thousands of visitors pack the racecourse on St Leger Day, many of them more interested in the stalls and marquees than in the racing. In the 1920s and 1930s it was not unusual for crowds of half a million to attend the four-day meeting.

Left: Queen Elizabeth at the St Leger meeting, 1950s. The Queen, in the light-coloured suit with her back to the camera, is a keen and knowledgeable racegoer. Her great grandfather, King Edward VII, was twice the owner of the winner of the St Leger.

Below: Doncaster Rovers, 1912. A large crowd of supporters surround the Doncaster Rovers football team in their horse-drawn wagonette after winning the Sheffield Challenge Cup in 1912. Note the boy at the front on the left with his hoop, known in South Yorkshire as a "bool" or "'barl".

SHEFFIELD

By the 1920s Sheffield had a population of more than half a million, eleven times its size at the time of the first national census in 1801. The city (it had achieved this status in 1893) had spread in all directions in the 19th century as a result of the continued growth of the light steel trades and the creation and rapid expansion of the heavy steel industry

ABOVE: The remains of **BEAUCHIEF ABBEY** in the Sheaf valley, founded between 1171 and 1176 by Robert FitzRanulf. Beauchief is a Norman-French name meaning "beautiful headland" that refers to the steeply wooded hillside beside the abbey.

ABOVE: **ECCLESALL ROAD,** *c* 1910. The view shows the road near its junction with Brocco Bank and Rustlings Road near Hunter's Bar. This very busy tram route not only led to residential suburbs but also to Endcliffe Park and Whiteley Woods, two of the most popular open spaces in the city.

ABOVE: **THE WICKER RAILWAY ARCHES, 1905.** The arches, which carried the Manchester, Sheffield and Lincolnshire railway into the town in 1845, are bedecked in honour of the visit of King Edward VII to open the new university.

LEFT: **HARRY BREARLEY**, discoverer of stainless steel in 1913. His ground-breaking discovery changed the face of cutlery manufacture after the First World War. He came from a poor Sheffield background, having been born in Ramsden's Yard, off the Wicker.

RIGHT: **SHEFFIELD SCISSORS-MAKER, EARLY 1900S.** Before the widespread mechanisation of the industry, cutlery and related trades were mostly in the hands of "little mesters" who ran their own businesses. Even when factories became common, little mesters rented spaces there. One or two little mesters still survive.

LEFT: **SHEPHERD WHEEL, EARLY 1900S.** The photograph shows the grinding of cutlery at this water-powered site in the Porter valley, which was first referred to in 1566. It was worked commercially till 1930 and until recently was open to the public by the city's museums service.

BELOW: **LOWER DON VALLEY, 1930S.** The fields of Sheffield's East End were covered between about 1850 and 1900 by the heavy steel industry. INSET: **CRUCIBLE STEEL SHOP, EARLY 1900S.** The development of crucible steel-making in the 1740s gave Sheffield an international reputation for high-quality steel manufacture.

LEFT: **ST PAUL'S CHURCH, EARLY 1900s.** The church was designed by members of the Platt family, the Rotherham mason-architects. The building of the church was begun in 1720 but it did not open until 1740. The church was demolished in 1938 and the site is now occupied by the Peace Gardens.

BELOW: **THE UNIVERSITY OF SHEFFIELD.** The Tudor-style buildings of the new university were opened by King Edward VII on July 12 1905. The commitment to gain full university status was spurred on when it was mooted that the University College of Leeds should become the University of Yorkshire.

ABOVE: **THE HOME GUARD.** The first volunteer in Sheffield was signed up at a police station within four minutes of the Foreign Secretary, Anthony Eden, announcing the formation of the Home Guard (originally called the Local Defence Volunteers) on the radio in May 1940.

RIGHT: **CORONATION PARTY, 1953.** The end of wartime hostilities and coronations were celebrated by street parties throughout the city, which included games, sports and dancing. This is the party in Rutland Street to celebrate the coronation of Queen Elizabeth II.

LEFT: **DARNALL CINEMA.** Opened in 1913, this cinema in Catcliffe Road was built by George Payling, a local builder. It closed in 1957. In its early years a good night out could be had at the "popular prices of 2d, 4d and 6d".

BELOW: **ABBEYFIELD PARK,** *c* 1910. Abbeyfield Park, a small park in Burngreave Road, was formerly the grounds of Abbeyfield House, which in the second half of the 19th century was the home of the Wake family. It became a public park in 1909.

ABOVE: **SHEFFIELD UNITED FOOTBALL TEAM, 1899.** The bowler- and top-hatted Sheffield United players show off the FA Cup that they had won decisively at Crystal Palace against Derby County before a crowd of 74,000, including the Prime Minister, AJ Balfour. Although behind 1-0 at half-time, a scintillating second-half display saw them score four times to inflict on Derby their second successive Cup Final defeat.

RIGHT: **SHEFFIELD WEDNESDAY FOOTBALL TEAM, 1907.** The playing squad and officials proudly pose with the FA Cup that they had won that year. In a tight game they had beaten Everton 2-1 at Crystal Palace before a crowd of 84,000.

Back Row (left to right) : Messrs. A. G. W. Dronfield, J. Holmes, A. J. Dickinson, J. C. Clegg, H. Nixon, J. Thackray, ——. Ellis, T. Lee, W. Turner, W. F. Wardley. *Middle Row* : J. Davis (asst. trainer), H. Newbould, H. Davis, Brittleton, Layton, Lyall, Bartlett, Slavin, Burton, Foxall, P. Frith (trainer). *Front Row* : Bradshaw, Chapman, A. Wilson, T. Crawshaw, Stewart, G. Simpson, and Maxwell.

ROTHERHAM

The town grew up on the eastern bank of the River Don where a low bluff provided a commanding site for All Saints' parish church. Industrial development began in the mid-18th century when the Walker Brothers established their foundry in neighbouring Masbrough. The iron-founding tradition gave rise to the town's railway engineering industry, stove grate industry and eventually its steel industry

ABOVE: **HIGH STREET,** *c* 1910. The photograph shows a weekday scene in the High Street with a mixture of traffic: a tram (the tramway system had been opened in February 1903), a horse-drawn cart, a private horse-drawn carriage, a cyclist and two boys pushing a sack barrow.

ABOVE: **BRIDGEGATE, EARLY 1900S.** This narrow street, before it was widened, must have been very busy on market days. There were drapers, boot-makers, hatters, a confectioner, pork butcher, chemist, stationer, tobacconist and even a basket-maker, pawnbroker and pianoforte dealer.

LEFT: **COLLEGE STREET, EARLY 1900S.** This busy commercial street on an important tram route had every type of shop at the beginning of the 20th century: chemists, tailors, drapers, watchmakers, fruit merchants, wine & spirit merchants, a hatter, a silk mercer and many more.

BRIDGEGATE, ROTHERHAM.

Left: **BRIDGEGATE, LATE 1940S.** In great contrast to the photograph of the same street in the early 1900s (opposite) is this scene photographed in the immediate post-war years, two decades after it had been widened and modernised.

Below: **MAIN STREET,** *c* 1910. The building is the new post office which opened in 1907 to replace the previous one that was in the old Westgate station from 1880. The elaborate set of telegraph poles above the roof are at the National Telephone Company's Rotherham exchange.

Above: **IMPERIAL BUILDINGS,** *c* 1910. In 1905 Rotherham Borough Council purchased the property on the north side at the top of High Street. The buildings were soon demolished and a new block of shops and offices, known as the Imperial Buildings, seen here from neighbouring Westgate, were opened in 1908.

Right: **DONCASTER GATE,** *c* 1920. This view is looking westwards towards the parish church with the Cinema House, with its Moorish-style architecture, and which opened in 1914, on the left.

Doncaster Gate, Rotherham.

RIGHT: **ANSTON BRASS BAND, 1925.**
Bands were formed in
Rotherham and the surrounding
villages in the late 19th and early
20th centuries. Rotherham even
had a mandolin band. This is
Anston brass band from the
villages of North and South
Anston.

BELOW: **BANDSTAND CLIFTON PARK,**
c **1910.** The bandstand was
erected in 1892 a year after the
opening of the park by the
Prince and Princess of Wales
(later King Edward VII and
Queen Alexandra). It was
removed to Ferham Park in 1919.
A new bandstand was erected in
1928.

ABOVE: **ROCHE ABBEY, EARLY**
1920S. Not a drink in sight
as the Women's Total
Abstinence Union pose for a
group photograph on their
outing to Roche Abbey in
July 1921. The abbey ruins
were a favourite destination
for club outings.

LEFT: **ORNAMENTAL LAKE,**
CLIFTON PARK, EARLY 1920S.
This was originally the
fishpond in the park
attached to Clifton House
that was bought by
Rotherham Corporation in
1891 "for the use of the
townspeople in perpetuity".
In 1892 the fishpond was
converted into a shallow lake
with an island in it.

G.172-2. The Swans, Clifton Park, Rotherham.   Copyright.   Scrivens

ABOVE: **VISCOUNT MILTON'S CHRISTENING, 1911.** An ox is being roasted at the christening of Viscount Milton at Wentworth Woodhouse on February 11 1911. The Viscount was the heir to the Fitzwilliam earldom. The celebrations were like a coronation with 7,000 official guests and 100,000 members of the public in attendance.

ABOVE RIGHT: **HIS FIRST MEET, 1913.** At less than three years old, in November 1913, Viscount Milton attends his first meet of the Wentworth Hunt. This is one of many photographs of the Wentworth estate and the Fitzwilliam family taken by EL Scrivens, the Doncaster postcard photographer.

ABOVE: **UNVEILING OF THE CENOTAPH, 1922.** Lt Gen Sir Ivor Maxse takes the salute at the unveiling of the memorial on November 26 1922 to the 1,304 local men who lost their lives in the First World War. The Bishop of Sheffield, Dr LH Burrows, is on the left.

LEFT: **CANAL TRIP, VE DAY, 1945.** A large group of children enjoying a boat trip on the canal at Aldwarke, just to the north of Rotherham, to celebrate Victory in Europe (VE) Day. This was a far happier occasion than one just over a century earlier, in 1841, when 50 people, mostly children, were drowned when a canal boat being launched at Masbrough capsized. It had been the tradition to allow children "to ride the launch".

BARNSLEY

For centuries Barnsley was a small market town with a wire-drawing industry. From about 1750 it began to expand through the growth of linen manufacturing and by 1851 there were 4,000 handlooms in 800 loomshops, mostly in cellars. In the second half of the 19th century linen manufacturing became a factory industry and went into a long decline, its place being taken in the town and the surrounding area by coal-mining

RIGHT: **CO-OPERATIVE STORES, 1952.** The photograph shows the drapery stores and offices of the Barnsley British Co-operative Society at the corner of Wellington Street and Market Street. The building was originally the "Central Premises" of the society, founded in 1862.

BELOW: **CRANE MOOR *c* 1900.** An evocative photograph of China Square and its inhabitants in Crane Moor, a hamlet in the "stone country" just over four miles south-west of the centre of Barnsley. The cottage walls are of stone, the roofs are of stone, and there are massive stone lintels and sills.

ABOVE: **WHITSUNTIDE, THURGOLAND, 1902.** Scholars, teachers, parents, family and friends of Thurgoland and Crane Moor Wesleyan Sunday Schools gather together in their Whitsuntide clothes outside the Green Dragon in Cote Lane, Thurgoland, for the Whitsuntide Parade.

RIGHT: **CHILDREN'S WARD, BECKETT HOSPITAL, *c* 1910.** Beckett Hospital, named after its founder, John Staniforth Beckett, was established in 1865 to provide medical services for the town's poor. The children's ward was opened in 1900.

RIGHT: **ALE & CAKE DAY, PENISTONE, *c* 1900.** The givers and recipients of ale and cake on Maundy Thursday pose for their picture. This ancient custom was discontinued in 1905. The first recorded instance of this almsgiving in Yorkshire was in 1210 at Knaresborough when King John gave money and clothes to 13 paupers.

Cheapside, Barnsley

LEFT: **CHEAPSIDE,** *c* 1910. This view, from near the bottom of New Street, shows how important a shopping street Cheapside had become. By the early 1900s such famous Barnsley names as Albert Hirst, pork butcher, Brady Webster, grocer, Edward Bailey, draper and milliner and Abraham Altham, tea dealer, all had premises there.

CHEAPSIDE, BARNSLEY. 30.

ABOVE: **CHEAPSIDE, EARLY 1920S.** The view this time is in the other direction towards Sheffield Road with the outdoor market on May Day Green on the left and the shops of Cheapside on the right.

LEFT: **BARNSLEY MARKET, MAY DAY GREEN.** The famous Barnsley market outgrew its original location on Market Hill and by 1900 filled May Day Green in two areas of canvas-covered stalls separated by Kendray Street. On market days, on Wednesdays and Saturdays, customers travelled from far and wide to snap up their bargains.

RIGHT: **MARKET HILL,** *c* 1910. In 1249 the Cluniac priory of St John of Pontefract obtained from King Henry III a charter for a weekly market in Barnsley. Market Hill was the original marketplace and was continuously used for a market from the 13th to the 20th century.

Market Hill, Barnsley.

Left: NEW STREET, EARLY 1900s. This view is from the bottom of the street towards the "Central Premises" of the Co-operative Society. The street became a busy shopping street. Of particular interest is the giant pair of spectacles above the premises of RE Gray, optician.

Below: EARLY BUS. The Barnsley & District Electric Traction Company began running tram services in the town in 1902. The first bus came into operation in 1912 and as it started to cover a larger area the company changed its name to Yorkshire Traction. By 1925 the company had a fleet of 118 buses.

Above: NEW STREET, c 1910. Another view of this important shopping street; this time the camera is pointing down the street towards Sheffield Road. The names of well-known Barnsley businesses are clearly visible: John Guest, JH Bailey and Lodge, the stationer.

Right: THE ARCADE, 1910. One of the most unusual and still surviving shopping streets in Barnsley is The Arcade linking Eldon Street and Market Hill. Walking and shopping in this glass-roofed, traffic-free arcade was a very different experience from the noise and crowds in the nearby open market.

QUEEN STREET, BARNSLEY

The Obelisk & Huddersfield Road, Barnsley.

ABOVE: **QUEEN STREET, EARLY 1930S.** This relatively modern view of Queen Street shows it in a state of change. On the left is the new store of Montague Burton, the tailor, opened in 1930. On the right the old premises, beyond Goodson's, would have gone by 1937 to make way for Marks & Spencer's store.

RIGHT: **HUDDERSFIELD ROAD,** *c* 1900. On the left is what became the Yorkshire Area Headquarters of the National Union of Mineworkers, built in 1874 for the South Yorkshire and Derbyshire Miners' Association. On the right is the obelisk, an elegant guide-post, which was removed in 1931.

BELOW: **PEEL SQUARE, 1930S.** The view is towards Eldon Street on the left and Queen Street on the right with Burton's tailoring store giving a modern touch to the scene. On the left is the beginning of Peel Street and on the right the beginning of Pitt Street.

PEEL SQUARE, BARNSLEY.

DONCASTER

Doncaster was the site of a Roman fort at a crossing of the River Don. In early medieval times it became a market town and in the early 17th century it became a centre for horse-racing. It expanded greatly following the decision in 1851 of the Great Northern Railway Company to establish its wagon and carriage repair workshops in the town. Coal-mining reached the area in the first decade of the 20th century and initiated further expansion

BELOW: **BAXTER GATE, EARLY 1900S.** Although there are no trams in this view, there can be no doubt that it was taken in the early 1900s: there are tramlines on the road and an ornate tram standard on the right. The first tram ran in 1902. On the left are the grand premises of Beetham's, wine & spirit merchants, erected in 1884.

ABOVE: **HIGH STREET FROM FRENCH GATE, 1920S.** Bustling crowds of shoppers throng the pavements and a policeman directs traffic at the crossroads of High Street, St Sepulchre Gate, Baxter Gate and French Gate. The clock at Clock Corner towers above the street junction on the left.

BELOW: **MARKET PLACE, *c* 1900.** A busy scene in the Market Place is shown, overlooked by the cathedral-like tower of the Victorian St George's parish church. Doncaster has been an important market centre since the Norman period, with the first market charter being granted in 1194.

ABOVE: **ROYAL DECORATIONS, 1912.** A final cleaning of the end of High Street takes place as the crowds gather on the morning of July 8 1912 amid the swags and flags in honour of the visit to the town of King George V and Queen Mary.

BELOW: **PROSPECT PLACE, 1935.** The date is May 6 1935 and the street has been decorated with streamers, Union Jacks and bunting in celebration of the silver jubilee of King George V. Of particular interest are the two little boys, one with a party hat, in their pedal cars.

A typical scene at Arksey during Floods. "Empire View" 65.

LEFT: **ARKSEY FLOOD, EARLY 1930S.** It is not surprising that villages, many of them only a few feet above sea level, in the Humberhead Levels near Doncaster, have suffered from periodic heavy flooding. The second part of the name Arksey means a piece of dry land surrounded by marsh.

BOTTOM, LEFT: **TICKHILL** AND BOTTOM RIGHT: **CONISBROUGH CASTLE, EARLY 1900S.** Doncaster is surrounded at short distances by attractive countryside and interesting historical sites which have long been the destinations of day excursions. Tickhill is a planned medieval town with a Norman castle and a magnificent Perpendicular parish church. The photograph shows its 18th-century market cross. The keep of Conisbrough Castle is one of the finest surviving pieces of 12th-century military architecture in the country.

473. CONISBROUGH CASTLE. ARJAY

First published in 2009 by Myriad Books Limited

35 Bishopsthorpe Road London SE26 4PA

Text copyright © Melvyn Jones

Melvyn Jones has asserted his right under the Copyright, Designs and Patents Act 1998 to be identified as the author of this work.

ISBN 1 84746 261 8
EAN 978 1 84746 261 9

Designed by Jerry Goldie Graphic Design

Printed in China

www.myriadbooks.com

With grateful thanks to Chris Sharp of Old Barnsley without whose help this book would not have been possible.

All photographs copyright © Sheffield Archives and Local Studies Library except:

Copyright © Joan and Melvyn Jones' personal collection
The cover (top left and right) and pages 3 (centre); 4 (centre right); 6 (top left); 7 (top); 8 (top, centre right and bottom left); 9 (top right); 10 (centre left); 15 (centre left and bottom); 16 (top right); 18 (bottom); 20 (centre right); 27 (top); 32 (bottom left and right).

Copyright © Chapeltown and High Green Archive
Page 6 (bottom left and bottom right); 8 (bottom right); 9 (centre left); 10 (top left); 11 (top left, top right and centre left); 12 (top left); 13 (bottom left); 14 (top, centre right, bottom left and bottom right); 16 (centre).

Copyright © Barnsley Local Studies Library
Page 2 (centre left); 4 (bottom left and right); 8 (centre left); 9 (bottom); 10 (bottom right); 12 (top right); 16 (top left and bottom); 26 (bottom right); 27 (centre and bottom right); 28 and 29 (all).

Copyright © Rotherham Archives and Local Studies Service
Page 3 (bottom row); 5 (centre); 9 (centre and inset right); page 11 (bottom); 13 (top and bottom right); 22 (top right and bottom); 23, 24 and 25 (all).

Copyright © Doncaster Local Studies Library
Page 3 (top); 5 (bottom left and right); 7 (bottom); 12 (bottom); 13 (centre right); 17 (all); 30 and 31 (all).